Discourses deli

the

Bliss Bytes Vol. 3

Nithyananda

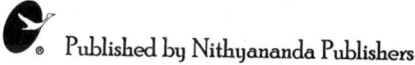 Published by Nithyananda Publishers

Encapsulations from discourses of Nithyananda.

Take one a day and be in Bliss.

The meditation techniques included in this book are to be practiced only under the direct supervision of an ordained teacher of Nithyananda Dhyanapeetam and in consultation with your personal physician to determine your fitness and ability to do the techniques. They are not intended to be a substitute for medical attention, examination, diagnosis or treatment. If someone tries these techniques without prior participation in the meditation programs of Nithyananda Dhyanapeetam and without the direct supervision of an ordained teacher of Nithyananda Dhyanapeetam, they shall be doing so entirely at their own risk; neither the author nor Nithyananda Dhyanapeetam nor Nithyananda Publishers shall be responsible for the consequences of their actions.

Published by:
Nithyananda Publishers
Nithyanandapuri, Off Mysore road
Bidadi - 562 109, Bengaluru
Karnataka state, India

Copyright© 2009 - 'Living Enlightenment' year

Previous Editions: 5500 copies
Fifth Edition: November 2009, 2000 copies

M.R.P in India only: Rs. 25 only

ISBN No.: 1-934364-38-X / 978-1-934364-38-3

All rights reserved. No part of this publication may be reproduced, or stored in a retrieval system, or transmitted by any form or by any means, electronic, mechanical, photocopying, recording or otherwise, without written permission of the publisher. In the event that you use any of the information in this book for yourself, the author and the publisher assume no responsibility for your actions. All proceeds from the sale of this book go towards supporting charitable activities.

Printed in India by
Judge Press, 97, Residency Road, Bangalore - 560 025, Karnataka
Ph: +91 80 2221 1168   Email: judgepress@gmail.com

CONTENTS

1. Our Nature is Aloneness 5
2. Truth Transforms 8
3. Respect Food, Waste it! 11
4. Morality is Skin-deep 14
5. Accept your Doubts and Move on 17
6. Let go of Procrastination! 20
7. Our Body Begs for Attention 23
8. Don't Miss the Miracles of your Life 26
9. Catch Yourself in the Act! 29
10. How to Create Your own Future 32
11. Multitasking is Mindless! 35
12. Heaven is NOW, Don't lose it! 38
13. What is Enlightenment? 41
14. Faith does Move Mountains! 44

15.	Experiment with the Truth	47
16.	Increase your Memory Without Effort!	50
17.	Can you Answer This?	53
18.	Do you Know what you Want?	56
19.	Relive and Relieve!	59
20.	Total Awareness leads to Enlightenment	62
21.	Devotion or Intellect, they Lead to the Same!	65
22.	Spirituality is an Intimate Experience	68
23.	From Non-violence to Vegetarianism	71
24.	What do you do When you do?	74
25.	Live from your Being	77
26.	Mysteries of the Universe are Miracles	80
27.	Liberation, Not Choices Brings Freedom	83
28.	Surrender alone brings Bliss	86
29.	There is No Ranking in Enlightenment	89
30.	Learn to Be in Bliss	92

not physically alone. To have aloneness, we need to do nothing. Aloneness is our reality. Only for material comforts, we need to work and struggle.

A disciple once asked a Zen master, 'How long does it take to be enlightened?'

The master said, 'Just the time it takes to blink your eye. You are already enlightened. You only need to declare it.'

The disciple asked again, 'What happened when your enlightenment came?'

The master said, 'Nothing. I decided that from that day, I shall live my enlightened state.'

People ask me, 'What will happen to my children, my business when I get enlightened?' I say: nothing; you will be better than what you are, in whatever you do. You will not go to an ashram or run away from your life commitments. Do not be afraid of your own transformation. There is no need to be afraid. Life will be so much more beautiful after the transformation.

2. Truth Transforms

I was twelve years old when I had my first spiritual experience.

It was Buddha poornima day (the day Buddha got enlightened). I sat on a rock below the Arunachala hill, deep in meditation. It was dusk. I was searching for the source of my thoughts within me.

Suddenly, I was jolted into a grand experience. I could see 360 degrees around me even with my eyes closed! Normally, we have only 120 degrees vision. But now, I could see all around me and above me and below me as well. I lost my identity; there was no 'me'. Everything was 'me'. I was the stones, the hill, the trees, and the sky. Everything in me vibrated with the feeling 'I am the universe'. I felt the whole Existence with the same sensitivity that I felt for my body. I was in complete bliss. Within 3 or 4 hours after the experience, I started moving and walking. The inner ecstasy continued for 3 days.

When I came out of it, my first thought was that a ghost had possessed me. It never occurred to me to connect it to a spiritual experience. I ran to an elderly *sannyasin* (female ascetic), who had a small ashram near the rock. She took care of me for a few days. She convinced me that I was not possessed by any ghost but possessed only by God; that it was a spiritual experience. I however never went near the rock for the next 3 or 4 months.

Soon, I was longing for the experience again. When I came out of the fear I started meditating earnestly. The search had begun. The longing to know the 'truth' took over me completely. I started to chase it.

I was about 13 years old when I ran away from home to North India in search of Truth. I had to come back after a while though because I was too young to cope with the hardships of such a life. But the urge to know the truth was so strong in me that I soon left home again. And this time for sure.

We cannot handle too much of truth. We can handle small doses well. Deeper truths start transforming us.

The ground on which we stand moves away. None of us really want to know the truth. Honesty and truths frighten us.

We cannot accept the truth and so we pretend, fantasize, and lie. We hide from the true self within ourselves. We know that we are not what we show ourselves to be. We even lie courteously.

Understand: only truth leads to enlightenment. Truth transforms us completely. When we invite truth into our life, we invite bliss.

3. Respect Food, Waste it!

Overeating is a modern disease.

People think that it is alright to eat more vegetarian food. Let us be clear here. Overeating is bad. Be it vegetarian or meat.

Overeating creates a lot of problems for us. We have never learnt to eat only what we need. We should be firm and eat only what we require and how much we need. We overeat because of our greed.

Vegetarian food is the best for people interested in spiritual practices. It digests easily and promotes good energy in our body. It helps in gentle energy flow connecting all the *chakras* or energy centers in our body. The compassion of Buddha led to the wide acceptance of vegetarian food.

A further refinement of vegetarian food is dining on what is called as *satvic* food. People on *satvic* vegetarian diet avoid jalapeno peppers, onion, and garlic. These vegetables contain steroids. They are all right as medicines and ingested in small quantities once in a while. Regular intake of these vegetables interferes with the energy flow in the *cakra*.

Overeating has the same effect as eating jalapeno peppers, onion, and garlic. When we overeat, we stuff food and make our body a trash bin. As if that pain was not enough, we end up wasting a lot of our body's resources in processing it inside us.

My devotees consider it a privilege to feed me. They pile my plate with many varieties of food. They expect me to eat it all up! They advise me not to waste it. They expect me to clean up the plate.

Be clear: wasting food outside is better. It is better to leave the food outside our body than getting the excess food inside our body. We will waste ourselves from within if we stuff ourselves with food.

When we decline the food in the plate, it remains outside. Others can share it. But, if we stuff ourselves with food, we are serving ourselves a double dose of harm. The excess food is wasted in the body. Our body has no use of it even as it sits in our body. We are exhausting our body's resources in processing it. If we overeat, food becomes a poison.

When something is consumed in excess, it becomes poison. The food, instead of nourishing, can become poisonous.

It is better to decline excess food than to consume it. Be aware of what and how much you eat! If you respect food, your body will respond by being respectful to you!

4. Morality is Skin-deep

Our concept of sin is a social concept. Our connotations of sin are social. Morality is a rule, a code. It is a way to cause the fear of sin in common man.

Every sincere spiritual seeker should have a sense of morality born out of his own understanding of what is right and wrong.

We should examine morality from the point of view of our own awareness. Let us not blindly follow a set rule or the dictates of the codes of morality created by society.

By following such codes blindly, we are causing more harm to ourselves than good. Such codes wound our Being. Our concept of morality has to be totally based on our understanding. Morality should not be carved out of greed or fear. Any morality based on greed or fear or social norms is only skin deep. It doesn't touch our heart. Our values don't shine from the depths of our Being.

A small story:

Three women died on earth and reached the court of *Yama* – the Lord of Death. Here, they awaited their final judgment to be delivered by Yama.

Yama asked the first woman, 'Did you lead a pure and faithful life?'

The woman replied, 'Yes, I led a very chaste life. I never even looked at a man other than my husband.'

Yama then checked her life record and verified the truth of her claims. He gave her a golden key and sent her to a special room in heaven.

Yama then asked the same question to the second woman. She replied, 'I have committed a sin by thinking of another man in my mind. However, physically, I have been pure and faithful to my husband.'

Yama said, 'I cannot treat you in the same way as I did the previous lady.' He gave her a silver key and sent her to an ordinary room in heaven.

When it was the turn of the third woman, Yama asked the same question. The lady replied, 'My Lord, I am an actress. I have done things that you can imagine and cannot imagine as well. I am quite prepared to accept any punishment you decide to hand me.'

Yama looked to the left and then to the right, and handed her a key and whispered in her ear, 'Alright, here is my room key!'

If we have been conditioned thoroughly by society, or are a religious fanatic, we will be furious at this story. However, if we are spiritual we will know that right and wrong, sin and merit, live only in our minds. Ofcourse, this is not a license to live as we please. Understand: morality has to happen in you as a mere byproduct of the right intelligence flowering in you. It is not to be imposed by any outer agency. An intelligent one will be moral automatically.

just let it be. Let everything and everyone be as they are or how they are.

The simplest way to enter aloneness is to bring in awareness. When we bring in awareness, we will be able to feel our real nature, our Self. It is very easy to slip into this mode, but the problem is we are afraid of it. So we resist it. So what happens is, even if we are alone physically, we will try to relate mentally with others and try to harbour some emotion or the other. Drop that habit.

When you are alone, enjoy your own self. Tell yourself that it is the best possible moment for you - to be with yourself. When you are with yourself, you can feel God best. Allow the aloneness to happen to you without resistance. You will then feel alone even when people surround you and when this happens, you will enjoy life as a grand drama while being yourself centered in the universal consciousness.

To start with, we need to experience physical aloneness. Once the joy of aloneness happens, once we experience the joy, it stays with us even when we are

1. Our Nature is Aloneness

We constantly live in the fear of facing ourselves. We are always busy, always asking 'what next' in the pretext of being busy.

In fact we are afraid and unhappy with ourselves. We think we are inferior to the next person, and superior to others. We never think or accept ourselves as we are. If we can accept ourselves as we are, we are in enlightenment.

We need to enter into a state of aloneness to reach bliss. This state does not mean that we reject our family or friends. We have to embrace aloneness and its beauty, with all of them around.

Aloneness is not loneliness. Aloneness is our inborn nature. Loneliness arises out of social conditioning. You feel lonely when no one is around you. You can be alone even when surrounded by people.

How do we reach this aloneness? If we try to search for aloneness we get into one more bondage. We should

5. Accept your Doubts and Move on

People ask me questions about the state of being enlightened. Some think that when enlightenment happens, they have to give up their family, friends, business, and their life will turn upside down.

The truth is that your lifestyle will not turn upside down. Your life will be more fulfilling, and you will enjoy everything in your life deeply.

People also wonder what it means to be enlightened. They ask me: is it the highest state of spiritual awareness? Were you materialistic before enlightenment and spiritual only after that? I tell you: there is no rule that you should be materialistic before and spiritual after. You can be spiritual before as well. Either way, you are greedy for something or the other - either material things or spiritual things, that's all. When you try to become *something*, it is material. When you try to become *someone*, you are spiritual. Until enlightenment, you are one or the other. Upon enlightenment you are as you are. You are enjoying everything; you are joyful; yet you are not attached to anything.

Enlightenment is not a state of mind. It is beyond mind. Do not bring words into this. Enlightenment is not anything.

An enlightened person always asks the question, 'what can I do?' They always want to know what they have to do. Their question always is, 'what can I do for you?' They are neither worried nor concerned about what others have to do for them.

This is a high-level technique what I am going to give you: do not ask for a method. It is simple. Follow it from today. Just tell yourself that you are enlightened. Accept yourself as you are. Don't think of improving yourself or improving someone else. Tell yourself: I am in the state I am supposed to be. Believe it deeply.

Be relaxed. Express your utter relaxation in everything you do. Tell your mind, your emotions, your being: 'I am enlightened'. If your mind expresses doubts, accept the doubts and move on.

Doubts are like a dog that barks at an elephant. Does the elephant even care? Doubts have no existence of their own. They will survive only if you feed them. Doubts will recede as you face them and accept them.

Change your entire focus to enlightenment. Realize that you are enlightened. Simply drop the idea that you should be or will be someone else when you are enlightened. Just accept whatever life brings to you. Accept that your mind has doubts; just accept that and move on.

Turn your mind inwards. Enjoy all the bubbles of joy from within. Watch your breath without controlling it and turn your mind inward. Enlightenment lies within. It is to be experienced, not to be analysed.

6. Let go of Procrastination!

We think that if have no bad habits like smoking, we are doing everything else perfectly right. Did you know that we all have a secret mental addiction?

This addiction leads us to do all kinds of things. We will deny that we have any addiction at all.

Listen now. We are addicted to postponing every minute. We have acquired the taste of postponing every task. We have created a mindset that allows us to put off everything. Yes, this is our secret addiction – procrastination.

Listen to the chatter of our mind. It is always busy collecting arguments, or listing reasons about why we should postpone some tasks. It has such power over us that we will never enter into the act itself. There are many things, for which we say we shall do that tomorrow. The tomorrow becomes another tomorrow and continues to grow and that tomorrow never happens.

We can accomplish a task if we decide to do it today. Some of us are skilled and confidant veterans in this game. We have tasks that will never get done, if ever.

A small story:

A man went to the master and asked, 'When will I become enlightened?'

The master said, 'Now.'

The disciple asked, 'Now? How can I become enlightened now? I need a lot of practice. It needs many methods. It needs hours of meditation. How can it be now?'

The master said, 'Never.'

Do you understand the story? It is the story of how the mind works or tricks us. If we think something can be done now, we have the power to make it happen now. If we think that something needs time, it will automatically take time, that's all. Remember this story whenever the mind says: you are not good enough. You are not complete by yourself. You are not full by yourself.

The mind will always tell us the same thing. It has always been telling us the same thing. Today our mind will say: *do that meditation, do this meditation, practice, practice this. Only then you will get enlightened,* and what not.

Tomorrow it will tell something different. It never lets us feel that we have reached somewhere or that we have achieved something. Couple this with the idea of procrastination and you have the perfect recipe for disaster.

This secret addiction that is procrastination is the root cause for all our problems like lack of confidence, anger, everything. When we procrastinate, we get into a lot of trouble and we end up with all these emotions.

Just decide today that you will not procrastinate. If you feel the tendency to procrastinate coming up, just ignore it and jump into action immediately. Show a red card to your mind. Once you taste life without procrastination, you will never procrastinate again in life.

7. Our Body Begs for Attention

We should understand one secret: *attention is energy*.

That is why it feels so good when somebody attends to us. When we are attended to, when somebody takes time to attend to us, when somebody serves us, we blossom! We even feel elated.

We can see that politicians seem to be always, continuously energetic. Do you know why? Everywhere, thousands of people listen to their speech. We can see that if the crowd is more, the volume of their voice will rise. It goes up because the attention creates more energy in them.

If we are well attended to, we feel energetic. We feel alive. When we do not live inside our body, when we do not attend to our body, we will feel that our body has shrunk. Our body really contracts, it shrinks. It just begs us, 'please give me your attention, please.'

This begging of our body is called pain. Pain is nothing but the begging of our own body asking for our attention; asking for our presence. Our body wants us to attend to it.

Why does our body do that? It is because we continuously live outside our body. Our body is here; but we are somewhere else. Our body is in the house; but in our mind, we are already in the office. When we are in the office, our mind is in the house. If we continuously live outside the body, our body will go without any attention. Pain is the way our body creates attention for itself. Pain is the way our body calls for attention when we don't attend to it properly. We need to understand one thing: pain is nothing but unawareness.

If we do not live with awareness in the 'now', 'here', our body will not be attended to. Our body will not have the attention of our being. When we give our attention, we will see that the pain simply disappears. When we do not live the real life, we will be only living with reasons. Our mind will be one way; our body will be in another way. And if we do not live truthfully, we create a new energy field around us called pain body.

Understand that if we continuously live in the past or the future, we are not present inside our system. When we are not present, the energy flow inside our system never happens totally and properly.

Attend to the 'now'. This state alone can confer upon us peace of mind, relief from worry and bliss. Be in the present, be pain free and blissful. This is the real enlightened state.

8. Don't Miss the Miracles of your Life

People ask me to perform miracles. I tell them that life itself is a miracle.

Consider a piece of bread transforming itself into a drop of blood inside your body. The bread that you eat becomes blood, is it not? Now, that is a true miracle! Thousands of such miracles happen in our body simultaneously. Life is the biggest miracle.

If this miracle is so obvious, why do we miss it? We miss all the wonderful, beautiful, and miraculous things that happen to us and our body, because we don't live in the moment.

The Buddhist monk Thich Nhat Hanh wrote a beautiful book 'Miracle of Mindfulness'. He shows how to appreciate life by living in a mindful state every moment. Only when you understand and appreciate that life is a miracle, it is worth living. As long as we do not understand life is a miracle, there is nothing much worth living for. This is one miracle that needs to be understood.

Being in the state of 'now', living in the present, brings us enormous power. You will understand and live in the power of now, when you understand that life is 'here' and 'now'.

When we understand the best way to lead life is to live in the now, it brings in tremendous healing effect and freedom. Not only do all the physical and psychological pains disappear, but we will also see a tremendous sense of freedom blossoming within us.

If we live in the 'now' and 'here,' we will neither bother about the next moment nor worry about the past. Because every moment is going be fresh to us, and we will always be in the 'now' and 'here' with no burden of the past or future.

Let us not make the practice of being in the 'now' and 'here' complicated. If we can manage 'now' and be 'here,' we can verily manage the next moment, which comes afresh as another 'now,' and 'here'.

Every moment takes birth only from this moment. Every moment takes birth afresh. It is born at that moment and dies at that instant. If we can live in this moment, we can also live the next moment. We will then live happily with no regrets, no guilt, no expectations and no surprises.

But how do we live today? We kill the moment we live in. In the same way, we kill the next moment and the next. As long as we do not live now here, we do not live in the present moment. We kill the moment. We kill life itself. We don't live it.

Let us live our miracles every second of it. Then you will see that every moment of your life, you become more and more sensitive to the real miracles of Life, to the way in which the universe or Existence is conducting the whole show. And when you tune in to this, everything becomes a miracle. It is then that you actually start enjoying life. It is then that you drop hankering for other material miracles and start seeing the real miracles unfolding every minute of existence. It is then that you start experiencing what the great masters have been talking about time and again.

9. Catch Yourself in the Act!

Everyday early in the morning, a Zen master would ask his disciples, 'How many of you have taken bath this morning?'

Almost all the disciples would raise their hands dutifully.

Next question would be, ' How many of you are aware that you took a bath when you took a bath?'

Not a single hand would raise.

Bathing is an act. But bathing with complete awareness is totally different. Today, surely all of us must have taken a bath and all of us must have brushed our teeth. But how any of us were aware of what we were doing when we did that?

When we brushed our teeth, how many of us were aware? When we took our bath how many of us were aware of the hot water falling on our body? Were we aware of our body after the bath? Did we feel rejuvenated after the bath? Did we feel relaxed after the bath? How many of us were aware of all these things when they happened?

A small story:

A king went to a master, and asked, 'Master, how can I become enlightened? Tell me about all the practices you do. What did you do to become enlightened? Please teach me the same techniques. I too want to become enlightened like you.'

The master said, 'Oh! I eat when I eat; I sleep when I sleep. That is all I do.'

The king could not understand.

The master explained, 'When I eat I only eat, I do not do anything else. Likewise when I sleep I only sleep, I do not do anything else.'

But what do we do? Just recall how we eat. We will either be watching television or reading a magazine when we were eating. Or it could be that we were talking to some one or continuously thinking of something. If by chance, we were calm, quietly sitting and eating, our spouse would have been there to report some problems in the house!

So in one way or the other, when we eat, our mind does everything except focus on the food and eating. We do everything except eat.

This is true even when we sleep! When we sleep, we do everything else except sleeping. Because, only when we sleep, we dream; nightmares and fear strokes happen. We have disturbed sleep. Whatever we do, we do everything else except that thing.

Try to catch yourself in the act. Become aware. When you become aware of what you are doing, there will be tremendous energy flow and intelligence happening in your system. This will set in motion a wonderful inner transformation.

10. How to Create Your own Future

There is a difference between imagination and dreaming. Do you know the finer aspects that differentiate the two?

Imagination and dreaming are not the same. They are two different things or states of mind. Imagination is creating something in the mind that is not there, for example, your own future. Creating that which is possible, not merely thinking about it, but also starting to work for it, towards it.

In imagination, you have a systematic, tangible, solid method. What does this mean? Look at it this way: if you can imagine yourself 10 kilometers ahead of the same route in which you are traveling, it is absolutely certain that you can reach there. This is imagination.

However, if you imagine yourself to be floating in the sky, it is a dream. Imagining that which cannot happen, just fantasizing, is in no way going to help you. Imagining events, which can happen in a creative way, can help you. This is called creative visualization.

Creative visualization has enormous power and will always help you in materialising things.

Dreaming is like fantasizing about your future. Just dreaming and fantasizing is in no way going to help you. I have seen many people fantasizing being with great actors and actresses. That is in no way going to help you. But imagining and planning your steps in accordance with your imagination will lead you to where you want to reach. This will undoubtedly be of help for you.

You can choose to live in dreams or in visualization. It is your choice. You have many kinds of freedom in your life. You do not recognize it, realize it or use it consciously. And you complain that you have no freedom.

One choice is, how to live. Another important choice is to decide how best to live. There is really only one choice for this. You can decide to live in the 'now', 'here', or be no where.

A small story:

A great master lived in Maharashtra. In the last phase of his life, for ten years, he was asked by doctors to eat only a certain type of rice and grains. Everyday he used to have the same type of food.

One day his cook was bored out of her wits. She told him, 'It is so boring to cook the same food. Are you not bored of eating the same food?'

The master replied, 'How can I eat the same food everyday? Once I eat, it is over. Every meal I feel it is a new meal. It is a new food!'

So, live in the 'now'. Live with imagination about your life, not with dreams. Dreams are called dreams because they will remain dreams till the end. Create your bliss with imagination that will materialize.

11. Multitasking is Mindless!

People think that it is more efficient to do two tasks together. That is foolishness!

Doing two tasks at a time is not efficiency; it is a deficiency. It leaves you unprepared to cope. Be clear: the moment you feel stressed it indicates only one thing – you are not living totally.

If you live this moment, you will never be afraid of other moments that will unfold during the day or in your life in the day or your life. Stress is nothing but psychological fear. Pure psychological terror is stress.

Look at how your life is now. As you do a task, your mind is continuously being boggled, burnt, worried, and anxious about the next moment. What to do? What to do next? What to do after this? And you think you are multitasking!

You mark these key words as a golden *sutra* - technique for your life. 99% of your worries never come true. The 1% that comes true is always for your own good! This statement is actually true. 99% of your fears and worries never come true. 99% of your stress is simply psychological terror.

You feel good if your enemy is too big, and bored if your enemy is too small. So, you know how to create stress. It is just a knack, an ability.

Be clear: when you decide to put your awareness on your mind, naturally you will understand how much stress you create on yourself. With awareness, all the stress will be healed. All the problems will be cleared.

However if you have been in pain and ignored it, then the pain body will be too big. If you put your awareness on your self, the pain body has to die. The pain body also wants to exist. It wants to protect its existence. It wants to survive.

To remain alive, the pain body never allows you to put your awareness on it. Try this. Turn your awareness on the stress. Look into it as deeply as possible. What is the source of this stress actually? When you trace its source, it will simply disappear!

Search throughout your body and mind with awareness. Whenever you get into a somber mood, whenever you get tired, whenever you get irritated, whenever you get angry, whenever you get the urge to shout at others, whenever you feel a headache, whenever you feel like giving headache to others, watch it.

Turn on your awareness. You will see that pain, fear, or stress melts like ice under the sun. Then, you can multitask in the real sense. What do I mean by 'real sense'? You can multitask with complete totality every moment. It will be efficient multitasking. Then it cannot even be called multitasking in your sense. It can be called simply 'living in the present completely'. When you live completely in the present, you become capable of doing many things at a time with complete totality every minute. This is what all great masters do in their fully enlightened state.

12. Heaven is NOW, Don't lose it!

As we go through our daily life and rituals, we constantly expect something better to come our way.

We decide, or dream, that when that better thing comes along, we will kick all the old things and move on.

Some people take this foolishness to greater heights. For example, they are tempted to consume alcoholic drinks, but they deny the temptation saying that they have a logic or reason for that. They say that if they do not take alcohol on earth, they are entitled for their share of *soma ras*, the divine nectar of Gods in heaven. This, they imagine, will happen after their death, when they are in heaven.

I tell them, 'Do not be foolish! Who has come back to tell us if the drink in heaven is better than the one on earth? Who knows that? Who knows if we will get a drink in heaven at all? And who can say if it is of the same quality or quantity?'

I am not telling you to drink. I am trying to make you understand that even as we lead our life on Earth facing its everyday challenges, we are thinking of what we will get in heaven. We think that what we are doing is a form of meditation or penance in order to catch a place in heaven.

This is the state of our life. We lead our lives expecting something better to come from somewhere, sometime, and through someone. The simplest and most profound problem this habit brings is that it stops us from living in the present. It completely obliterates our living here, on earth.

When we do this, we are setting up ourselves for a life of disappointment and stress. We think that we are going to get something better elsewhere. We are certain that an event of great significance will happen in a place far removed from where we are.

Drop it. Do not encourage these thoughts. Do not give up something with the anticipation of getting something better, something more.

If we believe that we are giving up something for a better thing, or exchange it for more than what we had, we are building anticipation. Often we think we are sacrificing something for a better thing, and that inexplicably eludes us. In the end, we lose all that we had. We lose everything.

Heaven is nothing but living in the present. Heaven is something to be experienced while you are living, not after you are dead. Heaven is living a liberated life. It is not any geographic location that is waiting for you once you die.

Let us cultivate the practice of living in the present. When we are totally in the moment, it opens up endless possibilities. Living in the present alone keeps us in Bliss ~ *Nithyananda*

13. What is Enlightenment?

We are always chasing happiness. We want to be happy all the time. The shortest way to be that way is to become enlightened!

Let me tell you what it means to be in the state of enlightenment. This is my personal experience.

The enlightenment keeps me in tremendous ecstasy 24 hours, 365 days a year. The word 'ecstasy' is not enough to describe the bliss I am in. Scientists say that whenever pleasure is stimulated in your system, a hormone called dopamine is released. Doctors call the point where it is released as the D-spot. When the chemical is released, our body is flooded with enormous energy.

When I am in the state of enlightenment, the idea of boundary, a limiting factor for most of us is lost. The feeling that my body ends here and the rest of the world starts here is absent. Everything is mine. The sensitivity with which I feel my body is the same that I feel for the whole cosmos.

My first experience with this kind of joy happened when I was a mere teenager. When I experienced it for the first time, the heightened sense of ecstasy lasted only for a few days. It gave me the first experience, the first glimpse. But after enlightenment, I live continuously in this heightened ecstasy. I am always in bliss day in and day out. It does not diminish, reduce. It just is. There is no time where I am not in this state.

When I became enlightened, I could no longer be judgmental. I only have compassion for everyone and everything. Merely by my physical presence, I radiate energy that will touch everyone.

With enlightenment, the basic idea of sex disappeared. The idea of being either male or female died. Though I have a male body, I can never identify with a male or female body. The truth is I am holding on to my body delicately, just like I hold a handkerchief, with my fingertips.

My mind doesn't exist. I am like a tape recorder that plays when it is switched on. When it plays, you hear the sound. When it is switched off, there is silence. Similarly, when I stop talking, a space is created. There are no words here. There is only silence.

There are thousands of enlightened masters living on planet Earth. Their energies are all one and the same. Only their expressions are different.

Let us all strive towards enlightenment. Let us all partake the ecstasy and bliss that is eternal. Let all of us be in *Nithyananda* – eternal bliss.

14. Faith does Move Mountains!

It is easy to acquire intelligence. If we work continuously using our intellect, it matures into intelligence.

Emotions arise from the heart. Ancient masters have developed many meditation techniques to work on our emotions. Any of these meditation techniques will change our emotions to faith.

Our thoughts have tremendous power. Be clear about one thing: if you believe in a particular God or Guru, believe in them with all your might. Do not bother about whether the God or Guru has power or not. Your faith has the power. An unenlightened master in whom you have faith can enlighten you!

A beautiful incident from the great Hindu epic Ramayana will help understand this idea better. Rama, the hero of the epic Ramayana, had to reach Lanka in order to rescue his wife Sita. Ravana, the demon king of Lanka had kidnapped Sita and taken her to his island kingdom.

An ocean divided the two kingdoms. Rama had to cross the ocean to enter Lanka. Rama decided that a bridge had to be built across the sea. Rama requested one of his devotees, Jambavan, the great bear, to oversee the construction of a bridge across the ocean. Rama asked Hanuman to fly across the sea to locate Sīta.

Hanuman said, 'Oh Lord, you are asking Jāmbavān to construct the bridge, but asking me to fly to Lanka. How can I do it?'

Rama replied, 'Hanuman, simply chant the name of Rama. With that alone, you will be able to accomplish the mission. Chanting the name of Rama is more powerful than my physical form.'

Hanuman did as he was told and flew to Lanka!

At a later stage in the same Ramayana epic, Hanuman, the greatest devotee of Rama, moved an entire mountain, the Sanjeevini mountain that housed medicinal herbs, to revive a stricken Lakshmana! The entire epic, Ramayana, is the song of the glory of

Rama. The name of Rama is so powerful that it provides tremendous boost to our faith. Through our faith alone, we can accomplish many things.

There are two versions of Ramayana: the Tulsi Ramayana by Tulsidas and Valmiki Ramayana, the earlier version. In the Northern part of India, especially in Gujarat and Uttar Pradesh, even the sweepers recite the verses of Ramayana, while sweeping the roads.

Faith has the power and remedy to overcome all our deficiencies. Let us cultivate faith in our favorite God or Guru. Then you will see that life becomes tremendously simple and enjoyable. Having faith does not mean having dependency. Real faith actually solidifies one's own being. That is what real faith does. People misunderstand it as dependency on another person. No! It actually solidifies oneself.

15. Experiment with the Truth

My search for spiritual truth began when I was about 10 years of age.

My family went to see Annamalai Swami, an ascetic and a close disciple of Ramana Maharishi, the great enlightened master who lived in my hometown, Tiruvannamalai, many years back.

I went there to listen to Annamalai Swami giving a discourse, although secretly I was waiting for the candy that he would give at the end of the discourse. Annamalai Swami was talking to a group of seekers. On that particular day, in his discourse, he was saying that we are not the body but something beyond it. He further explained that pain and suffering are beyond the body. They do not affect us. I forgot all about the candy.

I was surprised to hear this theory. I immediately thought, 'When my mother slaps me, I feel the pain. Then, why is he saying otherwise?'

His words continued to ring in my ears. I had an intense urge to experiment and verify his words. I ran back home, took a knife and cut my thigh with it. It started to bleed and I was in terrible pain. My parents were livid. They rushed me to a hospital. I still have that scar on me. After a few days, I went back to meet the Swami.

I said, '*Swamiji*, you told us that we are beyond the body, and pain and suffering don't exist. But, when I cut my thigh, it bled, and I had intense pain. Why?'

The Swami was surprised to hear of my experiment. He was very compassionate. He consoled me and taught me a simple meditation technique. All I had to do was to search for the source of my thoughts or see where my thoughts began. Though I had never meditated before, I decided to try it out.

Gradually, I realized that endless thoughts in our mind formed the first hurdle for spiritual growth. We all have problems with our thoughts. They seem to go one way when we want them to be another way. When we are at work, we are thinking about home. At home we think of work. When we greet people, we are thinking of something else. We edit when and what we speak.

Just be a little aware! If we are established in the truth, our inner chatter and outer chattering will disappear. All our thoughts and thinking will disappear. If we are completely truthful, we never have to think, we just need to *be* and relax. Why do we need to continuously think?

If we have to prepare continuously, whatever we prepare is a lie. When we speak too much, please be very clear that we are lying. We are hiding the truth. We are decorating a lie. Start becoming aware today.

Be aware! Be blissful! Experiment with the Truth I have told you just now and you will experience liberation from your very mind.

16. Increase your Memory Without Effort!

We are constrained by our mind. Our memory is like a library.

If we are attached to a single subject, thought, or memory, we will never have the freedom to access other memories or subjects. The world is filled with unlimited potentiality. Our minds and brains will be functioning at lower levels than they are capable of.

We need to have the emotional freedom from our memories. If we have total emotional freedom, we will have total access to any memory that we want. You can simply download any memory and start playing it instantly! There is a thumb rule for this process: No memory, when downloaded, should create any emotional bondage. Emotion filled memory is like a heavy video file; emotion free memory is like a light text file!

Remember, if we are emotionally free from any memory, we will be able to access and store any information we want from anywhere. People often ask me how to keep pace in this information driven world. It is hard to keep pace with the constant deluge of new information. My advice is the same. Don't create an emotional bondage with any memory.

Before enlightenment, I had read a few books about the *Upanishad* in Tamil. English was truly a foreign language for me.

After enlightenment, the entire scenario changed. I could access any language and information about various things in the past and present whenever I needed them. The moment I needed some information, it got downloaded. It seemed as if there was an encyclopedic CD package in my memory and all I had to do was to accesses it whenever necessary!

If we have an enlightened mind, there is no need for a formal education. Information will come seeking us! With my limited educational background and limited knowledge of English, I speak around the world. I give discourses and conduct so many classes. How is all this possible?

Ask the residents in my ahsram or close devotees about my schedule. I have a busy day. I hardly find time to read. So, where do I get all this knowledge? I speak to thousands of people all over the world. I answer so many questions. It is the enlightened state which causes this to happen.

Be free of emotional bondage. Be aware. Your memory will grow incessantly.

17. Can you Answer This?

We will ask many questions in our lifetime. The central question in our life is 'Who Am I?' The answer to this question is central to all our other questions. The other questions supplement and compliment this central question.

We ask many kinds of questions. Sometimes we question out of innocence, like a child, out of curiosity. Sometimes we ask questions just to exhibit our knowledge and ego. Sometimes we ask questions to check out if others are more knowledgeable. Sometimes we ask questions just to get an answer that will confirm our already formed opinions. Our questions just express our deep confusion about life, that's all.

A small story:

Laura, a teacher, was instructing the last class of the academic year. She prepared a few questions to get feedback from students on her teaching style.

One question in the questionnaire was, 'Have I influenced your attitude towards the subject?'

A student answered, 'No, I still like it.'

When people meet me, they start conversing with me about enlightenment and God. They begin to say that they wish to follow the spiritual path with my guidance. They ask esoteric questions on *karma* and *moksha*.

I change the subject. I talk about their personal lives, families, businesses, and what not. After even one hour perhaps, they never return to their original question on spirituality. It is because it does not matter to them really.

The fervor with which they started their spiritual queries was only to impress me with their keen interest and knowledge. Such fervor will not sustain. Their enthusiasm will evaporate rapidly.

'What is *Brahman*?' asks Arjuna to Krishna in the Bhagavad Gita. Krishna says, 'If I ask you to repeat the question, you would not even remember it!'

We ask questions about all external objects and issues; who is this, who is that? But we never turn our questioning inwards and ask, 'Who Am I?' If we are spiritual, we will be interested in asking ourselves, 'Who Am I?' It will answer all our other questions. The questioning attitude itself will dissolve. Our mind survives by questioning. Answers bring more questions.

Questions are the fuel for our minds. Unless we answer that central question, 'Who Am I?' we can never come out of the cycle of questions. An answer to one question will only lead to the next question.

Ask yourself this ultimate question, 'Who am I?' repeatedly. It will finally extinguish all your questions. The more we ask this question, the clearer we become in our mind. This is a direct path to bliss.

18. Do you Know what you Want?

We cringe when questions come our way. We are unable to handle them. This is because all our questions are unwanted. There will be only questions for each person that will lead him or her towards the experience of bliss. Because we are unable to ask that question, because we don't know that question, we ask all other questions and suffer.

Bliss or joy is grossly misunderstood. We equate it with the excitement of a new acquisition. Think of the excitement we have when we acquire something new - like a car or house. How long does it last? Not very long. Once we achieve the goal, the thrill and happiness disappear. This is not the joy or bliss that spiritual masters refer to.

Ramana Maharishi, a realized master who lived in the 20th century, defines this situation beautifully. He says, 'before we get it, even a mustard seed looks like a mountain; after we acquire it, even a mountain looks like a mustard seed.'

Do we know what we really want? Unfortunately, none of us do. We think we know. Are we happy with our success? No! We cannot be. We will never be. Till we know what we want, we will never be satisfied with whatever we achieve and acquire. Infact, at the end we will find that whatever we have acquired is of no value to us.

We are chasing desires all the time. This leads us into an endless cycle of desire and want. Most of these desires are not our own. They are borrowed from others. We see someone having or doing something and we want to do or have it. That is how things start. The possessive feeling, labeling things or relationships as 'mine' is the most dangerous trap that the mind can set for us. It is never ending, never fulfilling, always leading to suffering.

How can we end this confusion or suffering? We will continue to suffer and be disillusioned until we know who we are. Until we know who we are, the question of what we want cannot be answered! Understand that!

The smallest but greatest book ever is a book of sayings by Ramana Maharishi titled, 'Who Am I'. Let us dare to ask this question. This question will lead us into a long journey. Our question will transform into a quest. Our urge will become urgent.

We often think answers will end our questions or problems. I tell you, any question that is directional and leads to an answer will only add to your confusion. Only when the question leads us towards a solid experience will we really grow.

Awaken this intelligence, this bliss, this joy that is undiminished. Watching our mind is one way to awaken it. Vivekananda says, 'Till inner intelligence is awakened, no book will help you; once it is awakened you do not need any books!'

Address the question that arises from your being alone. That alone will take you in the path that is right for you. That alone will make you understand what you really want.

19. Relive and Relieve!

A devotee once asked me, 'How do we overcome *karma*?'

I replied, 'I will give you a simple technique. Practice it. From this moment, try and remember all the incidents in your life. Start going backwards from this moment until you reach your childhood days. Recall whatever you can. Don't bother about what you can't. You must realize that what you can't remember is really only a hangover. It has not deeply touched you. That is why it is not retained in your memory. Try this technique for a year. It will help you let go of your memories. It will help you to release yourself from *karma*. Reliving is a wonderful way of relieving.'

There is a qualifier to this exercise. We all can't go back and relive every memory. To do this totally, completely, we need to have the emotional freedom from our memories. It will work for us only if we have total emotional freedom, to recall any memory we wish to. No memory, when it is recalled, should create any emotional bondage or baggage. Only then are we emotionally free from them.

Remember: if we are emotionally free from any memory, we will be able to access and store memories anywhere. Don't create an emotional bondage with any memory. Release it.

Meditation is another useful method to control the influence of our mind. We can pass up anger, depression, and memories by meditation. Our body is nothing but the individual sparks of consciousness. Each spark in fact is a reflection of the Whole. Every spark makes a valuable contribution to the larger hologram or picture.

There is a technique simpler than meditation. It is to simply live moment to moment. Our life is lived moment to moment. Every moment gives birth to the next moment. If we can live this moment, then it is possible that we can live the next moment too. When we live moment to moment, we will live happily. We will have no regrets, no guilt, no expectations, and no surprises.

If we live completely in every moment, with total awareness, then we are in the state of eternal and causeless joy. Living in the moment, from moment to moment, is to live in the present, to live in the HERE and NOW, is what Buddha called mindfulness.

Live in the Now and conquer *karma*, memories, emotions and other energy blocks. Be in the Now and be enlightened!

20. Total Awareness leads to Enlightenment

Listen to this truth: the moment we imbibe a single dimension of the truth in any way, if we catch a single idea and imbibe it honestly, truthfully, we have caught the right thread. Just one aspect of the truth is enough. It can do wonders. There are so many paths that lead us to the ultimate truth.

Periapuranam, meaning the Great Epic, is a book in Tamil, which describes the life of 63 enlightened masters. If we study the life of these masters, we will be surprised. We will find that some of them have not done anything that seems worthwhile. In our opinion, they would have done nothing at all. They would have faced no challenges in their lives. Nothing remarkable would have happened in their lives. In fact most of them would have simply plucked flowers, offered it to God and achieved enlightenment! Understand: they all lived with complete devotion and awareness towards God. So that was enough. We may claim the same thing of ourselves but it is not true. Our minds are too complex to be able to do this. In those days it was possible.

What we do is not important; what matters is how honest we are with our actions. When the masters offered flowers, they were true and honest in their action. We also offer flowers everyday and do all possible things to please God but we are not enlightened as yet.

It is because we are not honest. When these masters pluck flowers to offer to God, they are thinking of Him to whom they are offering the flowers. They are totally devoted to the thought of the deity with nothing else distracting them.

When we pluck flowers, even if it is to offer to our favorite deity, we are thinking of something else, somebody else. I have seen people who do rituals regularly. During the ritual, they will be thinking of something else. Their thoughts will be either with their office work or some thing else in their life.

Enlightenment leads to thoughtlessness. I was traversing the Omkara hills on *Buddha Purnima* night when I had my ultimate spiritual experience-enlightenment. It was a full moon night and I was sitting on the banks of the river Narmada, totally relaxed. I had given up all my meditation techniques, *mantras* and penance, just a week earlier. I decided to relax totally and let go of everything. I simply sat and enjoyed nature's beauty. Around midnight, the relaxation became deeper and deeper and the thoughts became less and less. The inner chattering totally stopped and an unimaginable ecstasy took over me. There was no body, no boundary. I became one with the cosmic energy, the Divine. I became forever blissful.

Our being knows the truth. We only need to open our hearts and minds to it. Once we begin to live in the truth, we will expand and cover the entire universe.

21. Devotion or Intellect, they Lead to the Same!

The words *created, creator* and *creation* cause unending arguments.

Let us be clear. What we actually see as three separate entities are not separate at all. The creator, created and creation are all the same! The words mean the same thing!

Creation itself is intelligence. Creation has its own intelligence to direct its growth. The creation is continuously creating. Only the creating exists. Only the process exists.

Where does this concept fit in our ultimate goal, which is to live joyfully? To be joyful, we need to learn to live without the help of body and mind.

Many devotees ask me, 'What is destiny?'

I answer, 'Your present is a totality of all your past decisions and your future is the totality of all your present decisions. The purpose of human life is to learn the techniques to live blissfully, without the help of the body and mind. Learn that. That is what I mean by *being with God*.

Learn to live in ecstasy. Great masters like Ramana Maharishi, Adi Shankara and Swami Vivekananda were great intellectuals. Ramana said that learning to live ecstatically, blissfully without the help of the body and mind is the only thing we have to learn because it is the ultimate goal.

Our understanding of the types of *Bhakti yoga* and *Gnana Yoga* is flawed. We think that *Bhakti yoga* primarily means devotion, and *Gnana Yoga* means wisdom, an intellectual process. We are wrong.

Bhakti yoga and *Gnana Yoga* are means by which we unite with the Divine. Masters like Ramana Maharishi, even though intellectual, expressed *bhakti* at its peak. Two other great masters Chaitanya and Ramanuja also expressed their great wisdom through *bhakti*. Ramanuja's commentaries on the scriptures are incomparable. Both are intellectuals, but are perceived as *bhakti* proponents. Be clear: there is no difference between *Gnana* and *Bhakti* yoga.

Devotion or faith is an easy way to attain liberation or enlightenment. But even if we have faith, nobody can liberate us like magic. We each have to liberate ourselves using the power of faith. We have to work on ourselves.

This is the way to acquire enlightenment. When we work on ourselves, and when the Guru's grace descends on us, we get enlightened.

Both these paths are not different from one another. In our journey to enlightenment, it is not important which path we travel; what is important is how sincerely we travel.

22. Spirituality is an Intimate Experience

Everything about spirituality is personal, intimate, and quiet. This is the exact opposite of how the outer world functions.

My spiritual experience is more intimate than a love affair. Consider this: spiritual experience is beyond a conventional love affair that takes place in the world around us. A love affair takes place between two people. Here, I am talking about an experience without duality. It is an experience between one and the same one. Is there a name for this in the outer world? This experience is called enlightenment in the spiritual world.

Do you talk about your love affairs to your acquaintances? If you do, then probably you have developed a certain degree of intimacy with that person. Else, you cannot open up.

Someone I recently met told me, '*Swamiji*, I have one problem. I am not yet comfortable with you. We have just met each other. I know you since a short time. So, I cannot completely accept everything you say.'

Let it be clear: you all might not be able to accept whatever I say. You may question me since you have doubts about the truths I bring out. I have no proof or certificates for the experiences I had. It is a deep subjective experience. So, it will be difficult for you to feel it.

Maybe you cannot believe what I say. Many of you may not believe what I say regarding my spiritual experiences. It is fine with me. You can listen to it and forget all about it. I often narrate my spiritual experiences for the sake of a few sincere seekers. These sincere seekers are interested to know the truth. I narrate my earliest experiences for them.

Even to those who do believe, my experience is *my* truth; it does not apply to them. They will have to experience their own truth for them to express it in their words. Each one's experience is an intimate affair.

Every seeker has a different experience. It is an intimate and personal affair. Everyone searches for that undiminishing, undivideable, happiness. Everyone is looking for happiness, joy. The occurrence of joy is the experience of energy. This experience of energy in your body is called enlightenment. It is this enlightenment that leads to everlasting bliss, *Nithyananda*.

Walk inwards. The journey is long and difficult only if you think it is. But whatever may be the case, it will yield only the best results! Have faith in this statement and start your intimate love affair with the Divine!

23. From Non-violence to Vegetarianism

Ideally, we should all be masters of free will. Our actions and decisions should be independent of the idea of punishment or reward.

I call this morality from within. This value springs from the depths of our being, from the core of our own consciousness. This does not feel artificial or forced. However, if we try to follow the rules and regulations for social life, we will feel constrained and bound by them. We simply want to try and escape from them.

In spirituality, nothing can be labeled as right or wrong. There is no thumb rule that distinguishes the right or wrong. There is also no rule that dictates what is right and what is wrong.

Yet, when we live in society, we all follow certain rules to have a peaceful and happy social life. We have an unspoken agreement amongst ourselves. The agreement is something like this: don't try to kill me and I will not try to kill you. That is the social law.

It is only because of this binding law that we adhere to morality. If we know that we are not going to be punished for killing someone, we will not hesitate in killing others! This is the truth. Forced morality gives rise to this kind of an understanding.

Ahimsa, or nonviolence is one of the best universal principles. This principle lets us live harmoniously with others. The principle of *ahimsa* can be applied to the food that we eat. In my opinion, the idea of vegetarian food must have developed from Buddha's time. He was so compassionate and believed strongly in *ahimsa*.

Ancient sages do not mention the word or the concept of 'vegetarianism'. Even in the Upanishad, where ways of living for spiritual people are described, there is mention of only *satvic* food - vegetarian food.

Right from my birth, I have always been a vegetarian. I have never tasted meat, eggs or fish. I know how the body works with vegetarian food. Vegetarian food increases the joy and sensitivity in your energy flow. You will feel light and ecstatic. Vegetarian food is the best choice for people who want to take up the spiritual path or meditate.

When you follow the path of *ahimsa* and vegetarianism, you will find yourself softening and becoming sensitive to Existence that is embracing you. You will find that you fall very easily in tune with the Cosmic Energy.

24. What do you do When you do?

Do you know that when we sleep, we are actually not sleeping? We will not know how to sleep well until we learn to live in the 'now'.

Psychologists say that a person living in the Western countries never sleeps for more than 14 minutes at a stretch; more often it is less. After 14 minutes, he comes back to the dream state or wakeful consciousness or just floats in the dream level. Again he goes back to sleep for a maximum of 14 minutes. Then he comes back to the dream level. Again he goes back to sleep. They call this the rapid eye movement or REM sleep pattern.

We never sleep totally even when we sleep. There are levels of the mind in which we never have dreams. We never need to have any dreams. We can directly enter into deep sleep, if we know how to live in the 'now', the present moment.

If we know how to live in the 'now', we will know the art of eating, the art of sleeping, and the art of doing everything the right way. That is the art of living.

Can we try to remember one incident from our day in complete detail? No! We are more dead than alive. We almost live like a man in half sleep. We do things without fully knowing what we do. Do we recall brushing our teeth ever? Do we remember the sensation of the cold water in our mouth when we brush? Do we remember the taste of the toothpaste in our mouth or the pressure of our toothbrush upon our gums or how we felt after brushing? Or how the water felt when we poured it on our body in the shower? Have we ever wondered how the whole thing happens? Do we ever wonder what happens after we have eaten our food?

Look at our life; look at our faces. We look bored most of the time. Somehow we are pulling along. The juice or the joy or the pep of life is not there in us. It is just a drag. Why? Because all we do, all that we know to do is how to postpone enjoyment of the moment.

Our mind never sits with our being. Our mind never lives the moment. Our mind never lives in the same moment that we are in. We are always in the space of tomorrow or in the space of yesterday. It is never in the space of today, 'now', the present.

Live in the present. This is the secret of the art of living.

25. Live from your Being

If I ask you, 'What did you eat for breakfast,' some of you might be able to say a few things you ate. But if I ask you how it tasted, you will have no answer.

The truth is, you are always in a hurry. Your tongue never tastes the food when you eat. Your eyes never see when you look. Your ears never listen when you hear. Your body never feels when you touch.

Consider the simplest of things you do. Consider shaking hands with people or visitors. How many times do you shake your hands in a bubbling way? For you it has become a mechanical action. Your hand is practically a dead man's hand. Your handshake is a dead man's handshake. All you do is, stretch your hands; you never stretch your being. Never has your inner being penetrated through it.

How does one do anything from one's being? The answer is simple. Be in the truth. When you live in the truth, if you are truthful in thought, word and deed, there is no need to prepare a script, or hold a mental rehearsal, or decide how to say something to another person.

Consider the many ways in which you lie everyday. When there is no truth in you, it will reflect in your actions. That is the simple reason why almost all love affairs end in failure. How long can you continue to act? How long can you keep on preparing? How many times? How many days? How many times can you remember what you said the previous time? Not more than once, certainly.

The truth will come out eventually. And when it comes out, you start feeling uneasy and start another round of lies. Whe I say lie, I dont mean the gross lies that you speak. I mean the subtle lies that you talk, act and do every minute unconsciously to hide the truth from expressing in you. Every minute, you resist being relaxed inside the truth; that is the problem.

Because no one is really relaxed in the truth, everyone feels unconsciously cheated in some way or the other. The woman says you have cheated her. And you say she has cheated you. Both feel cheated by the other. In reality, nobody is cheating. It is just that your true nature or reality suddenly emerges and you feel grossly disappointed about something you can't really express.

A love affair is like a dye and powder. When you go in the rain, the color changes as the dye runs. Black runs into white and white into black. How long can you maintain the pretense? Naturally, the truth has to come out. The truth comes out when you relax. After that, you find yourself in big trouble. But there is no need to panic. Truth is the best thing that can happen to you.

Fall in tune with the truth. This way, there will be no need to remember *what* you said *when*. Then there will be no problem. Then there will be no fear of having to create any script. You can live as you are.

Live in the truth. That is the easiest way to eternal bliss!

26. Mysteries of the Universe are Miracles

Precognition is a common experience for most of us.

Let us say for example, that we feel that a particular person is about to call us. Sure enough, when the phone rings, that person will be on line!

Suppose we are watching the television show. Suddenly, we know what the character will say next. Sure enough, that character mouths the words as if to oblige us.

Another experience: let us assume that we are ready for dinner. Precisely then, the doorbell chimes. Even before we open the door, we know who is at the door. We expect a friend we haven't seen in years. Sure enough the friend is at our doorstep!

In my discourses, I often ask the audience if they have experienced something similar at some point in time in their lives. Over 50% of the audience confirms having had this expericnce every time.

When it happens, we ignore it. In fact, most of the time, we brush it aside as a coincidence. When this happens repetitively with a person, we attach the tag 'gifted'. In fact, we attach 'gifted' label to those who see auras and sense the vibrational energy of people and places.

For any experience to be termed as a 'gift', the magnitude and frequency of the experience should be consistent. It should be far greater than mere chance for us to stop calling it a coincidence.

In real life, we come across people making many predictions and forecasts. Some can accurately predict disasters, time and again; others give exact forecasts of deaths; many can heal people, who have been given up by doctors; some can produce substances out of thin air. We have a single word for all of these happenings - miracles.

We differentiate between coincidences and miracles depending on the degree of unexpectedness of the incident. These incidents, where we don't see the causal linkage, we call miracles. Scientific laws cannot explain miracles. When Science cannot explain a phenomenon, it is simply labeled as barbaric or miraculous.

There are no miracles in life. It is simply that we don't yet understand the laws that govern occurrence of such incidents, which seem to defy 'scientific' laws.

First, we need to accept and understand that the universe supports laws that go beyond the 'scientific' laws discovered by humans. This basic acceptance will lead us to the next level, to understand the cause and effect linkages behind many of these inexplicable happenings. Then, we begin to deeply appreciate the mysteries of this grand universe.

27. Liberation, not choices brings freedom

We all attend discourses delivered by realized masters. We listen to everything they say. We agree or we disagree, and we go home.

Once home, we forget all about the discourse. For a lasting change to take place, we must be able to internalize the key points in the discourse. We must remember, recall, and practice at least some of the key points of the discourse.

We need ways to remember what was said at the discourse. The question and answer session at the end of each discourse is a way to clarify doubts.

The question and answer session is like dining in a restaurant. Everything I have presented to you is like a series of choices. They are like the items on the menu card we hold in our hands. We have several choices here. First, we have to decide if we want to eat. If we want to eat, then we must decide if there is anything interesting in the menu presented to us. Once we make the choice, we can eat the food of our choice.

Similarly, in a discourse, I touch so many topics. It is our choice to internalize them. We can select the best method. We can seek clarifications for our doubts in the question and answer session. Again, the choice to implement and internalize it is completely up to each individual.

We have choice in everything we do. We have the choice to follow the truth or ditch it. We have the choice to cling to our lies or banish it. We can make the choice to follow the master or not. We have to be honest about the choices we make.

A great truth supercedes all our choices. We need to recognize that truth. Of course, the truth does not care whether we believe in it or not. It simply exists.

The great truth is that we are all connected. We are connected at the physical, mental, and spiritual levels. We are each not individuals or islands as we think we are. We cannot be. We are all interconnected with each other like the pieces of a puzzle.

Another great truth is the experience of enlightenment.

How much of this great truth are we willing to allow to operate on our lives? That is a matter for each one of us to internalize and examine. Are you game? Ask yourself. Answer consciously. Work towards it.

28. Surrender alone brings Bliss

We are interconnected through our bodies and thoughts.

The moment we understand how deeply, totally, and intensely connected we are, we will open many new dimensions of living. We can experience bliss. This is the ultimate spiritual experience.

Every day in our lives, we are stressed. We are continuously disturbed. We think that we have too much to do. We think that we have one body, one small body, to think or enjoy. And the troubles and trials the body faces everyday is too much for some of us. All our troubles melt away when we disappear into the collective consciousness.

When we disappear into the collective consciousness, we will have so many dimensions, so many possibilities. These are unimaginable now. Sometimes we have so much fun, so much joy bubbling within our body. Suppose we have two bodies, imagine how much joy can pour forth from it. Being in the collective consciousness, disappearing into the collective consciousness, is simply multiplying that joy many fold! It is something like having three different bodies in three different continents living in different cultures. The joy derived from each of them is all the same. The bliss or joy of living in the collective consciousness is beyond all these.

When we completely experience that we are consciousness without boundaries, it is an inexplicable experience. It is difficult to imagine or visualize the experience.

At the end of the programs that I conduct, I have seen people filled with ecstasy. In their exalted state of ecstasy, they forget their name, identity, social status, education, qualifications, wealth, and religion. They forget everything. They forget who they are and what they have. They simply begin to look at each other with great respect, as a microcosm of the universe! They start respecting the other effortlessly. They fall at each other's feet with no second thought!

I have seen a father-in-law fall at the feet of his daughter-in-law. In India this never happens. It is too much to ask for from the traditional people. But this has happens at the end of our programs. They do it because they get a glimpse of the divinity in the other person at that moment. The mother-in-law sees the divinity in her son-in-law and falls at his feet! A grandparent touched the feet of a granddaughter. The bosses touch the feet of their staff.

We need to go layer by layer, level by level, to realize that we are a part of the collective consciousness. We each are a part of the collective consciousness. Think about this concept. Meditate on it. It will cause radical changes in you.

29. There is No Ranking in Enlightenment

Samadhi is the state of enlightenment. It is an irreversible experience, which signifies the union of the individual Self with the collective consciousness.

Samadhi in Sanskrit refers to the state that is our natural and original state, the state of divinity.

Make no difference or distinction between different states of *samadhi* as superior or inferior. There is no substitute to the ultimate experience.

A small story:

Three thirsty strangers come to a tank in the middle of a village. They are about to enter the tank, when one person asks the others, 'Is this drinking water? I am thirsty.'

Another one replies, 'I don't know about water. But I know this is *pani* (water in Hindi language).'

The third man says, 'I know this is *thanni* (water in Tamil language).'

The fourth man, the local villager, is upset with all these names that he hears. He says, 'This is *neeru* (water in Kannada language). I know it because my grandfather built this tank.'

Even before entering the tank, the four men start fighting with each other. Before anyone could stop them, they hurt each other. Had they been patient and entered the tank, they would have realized that they were all speaking about the same thing!

With a little bit of patience and understanding, anyone can drink the water; anyone can experience the bliss. Once we have experienced the bliss, we can also supply it to everyone around us. What a wonderful gift this experience can provide! We can continue to experience the bliss and radiate it to everyone else. Bliss has no other meaning or name.

Enlightenment is not about verbiage. It is not about concepts, principles and philosophies. It is the awareness of the ultimate truth. It is an experience.

It has been said by all great masters that one who has experienced cannot express that experience and one who expresses could not have had the experience. All these people who endlessly argue about the states and stages of enlightenment and *samadhi*, have no idea what they are talking about. They misunderstand and mis-communicate the words of great masters who have hinted about their ultimate experiences.

Enlightenment, be it *samadhi, satori, moksha, kaivalya, or nirvana* is just one ultimate experience. It cannot be graded. It is eternal bliss - *Nithyananda*.

30. Learn to Be in Bliss

We are filled with negative thoughts and emotions most part of our lives. Negativity leads to suffering. We then wonder why we are suffering.

We can control anger and depression by meditation. Just by analyzing the seven *chakras* that are in our body, and the individual consciousness, we can remove negativity and control the mind. The seven *chakras* are major energy centers in our body that influence our wellbeing at the physical and emotional levels.

We are like an onion. A human body is made of many energy layers. Just like we peel an onion layer by layer, we need to explore the layers of our body. Let us peel away all the layers of the onion. What do we find inside? Emptiness. The onion, which looks solid, feels solid, when opened layer by layer, reveals its emptiness finally.

Similarly, each of us thinks that we are individuals. We think that we are individual consciousness. But when we begin to peel the layers of individual identity, we find nothing inside. What we will find therein is the collective consciousness. Remember this always. This will help us prevent anger or depression. It reminds us that there is no room for anything – thought or feeling, sneaking into us from others, through others, by others.

The collective consciousness is an experience. This science is no longer taught. Unfortunately, enlightened masters did not create the modern education system. The education system designed and developed by the ancient sages of the East, the *gurukul* structure, is 'now' extinct. It is no longer practiced. The tradition has long since died.

That is why we suffer despite being educated. We suffer throughout our life. In childhood, we are always taught that we are separate from others. In school, we are taught that we are somebody unique. Then, as adults, we are taught to compete with others. All this education goes in destroying the feeling of collective consciousness in us.

The truth is that we are all one. We are bliss. We each mirror the collective consciousness. We have lost touch with this truth. That is why I conduct meditation programs every week all over the world. I am doing this continuously. We are doing this continuously as there is no *gurukul* system alive today. The ancient system of education does not exist any longer.

If we can change the way we educate our children, different from the way we have educated ourselves, without judgment, without comparison, without competition, with our focus only on learning about the truth, and experiencing the truth, we can teach them to live without suffering. We can be in eternal bliss, *Nithyananda!*

About Paramahamsa Nithyananda

Paramahamsa Nithyananda is an enlightened master living amidst us today. With a worldwide movement for meditation and inner bliss, Nithyananda offers solutions for situations as practical as every day stress to the quest for something as profound as enlightenment. He left home at a young age and traveled the length and breadth of India, visiting holy shrines and associating himself with spiritual masters and mystics. He realized his intrinsic knowledge through the paths of meditation, yoga, tantra, knowledge, devotion and other Eastern metaphysical sciences. With an enlightened insight into the core of human nature, Nithyananda has defined his mission for humanity at large. Rooted in the ancient tradition of living enlightenment, and embracing all world religions as sacred and unique, Nithyananda draws people from around the globe, crossing all societal, cultural, language, age and gender barriers.

About Nithyananda Mission

Nithyananda Mission is a worldwide movement for spreading meditation and inner bliss. The services provided by the organization include • meditation • yoga • corporate leadership programs • free energy healing through the *Nithya Spiritual Healing system* • free education to youth • promoting art and culture • *satsangs* (spiritual gatherings) • free medical camps and eye surgeries • free meals at all ashrams worldwide • a holistic system of education for children through the ashram *gurukul* and a host of specially designed meditation programs.

Programs Offered by Nithyananda Mission

Inner Awakening

Inner Awakening is a 21-day 'master' program that is intensely transformative. It is designed to reproduce all the components of *jeevan mukti* or 'Living Enlightenment' in every individual and brings about an irreversible alchemy of moving from the mundane to the Divine.

Life Bliss Engineering (LBE)

LBE is a 90-day residential program to experience the intense and transformative power of being in an enlightened master's presence. Conducted at the Bengaluru ashram in India, it takes you to the depths of your being through yoga, meditation and a wide range of multifarious activities and helps you to awaken your innate peak potential. It is a lifetime opportunity to learn directly from a living enlightened master, to engineer your very body and mind for enlightened living.

Kalpataru

A one-day meditation program that sows in you the seed of Living Enlightenment. This program empowers you with the energy to **align your actions with your intentions** so you move with outer world success and inner bliss.

Contact Us

USA:

Los Angeles
Life Bliss Foundation
9720 Central Avenue, Montclair, CA 91763
USA
Ph.: +1 909 625 1400
Email: programs@lifebliss.org, shop@lifebliss.org
URL: www.lifeblissfoundation.org

MALAYSIA:

Kuala Lumpur
14, Jalan Desa Gombak 5, Taman Desa Gombak
53000 KL, MALAYSIA
Ph.: +601 78861644 / +601 22350567
Email: murthi.kasavan@gmail.com,
manirantaraananda@gmail.com
URL: www.mynithyananda.com

INDIA:

Bengaluru, Karnataka
(Spiritual headquarters and Nithyananda Vedic Temple)
Nithyananda Dhyanapeetam,
Nithyanandapuri, Off Mysore Road,
Bidadi, Bengaluru - 562 109
Karnataka, INDIA
Ph.: +91 97422 03311 / +91 92430 48957
Email: mail@nithyananda.org
URL:www.nithyananda.org

Visit www.nithyanandagalleria.com or www.lifeblissgalleria.com for more information.
E-mail: nithyanandagalleria@gmail.com & shop@lifebliss.org

Over 500 FREE discourses of Nithyananda available at http://www.youtube.com/lifeblissfoundation